THE SILENT ONES

poems by

Michael B. McMahon

Finishing Line Press
Georgetown, Kentucky

THE SILENT ONES

Publisher: Leah Huete de Maines

Editor: Christen Kincaid

Cover Art: Wolcott, Marion Post, photographer. Guests of Sarasota trailer
park, Sarasota, Florida, picnicking at the beach. Jan. Photograph. Retrieved
from the Library of Congress, <www.loc.gov/item/2017806306/>.

Author Photo: Jolyne S. Daughtry

Cover Design: Elizabeth Maines McCleavy

Order online: www.finishinglinepress.com
                also available on amazon.com

Author inquiries and mail orders:
Finishing Line Press
P. O. Box 1626
Georgetown, Kentucky 40324
U. S. A.

Table of Contents

For my gracious advocates: Ruth, Jody and Catherine

I.

Chalmers Lane

I would squat on the curb
and whittle a blunt stick
until it was sharp enough
to fell a brontosaurus.
Bricks underfoot,
yellowish-orange, were laid
by men like Dominic
whose trowel fluffed the mortar.

On hot July days
the cartilage of tar
that cushioned those bricks
would break out in boils.
I could fingerprint myself,
come back weeks later,
point to the whorls.

After dark, when
the air grew cool
I'd go down on my knees,
chest and face to borrow
the bricks' lingering warmth,
laying it by
for times I did not know.

Headwaters

The rising wash of flotsam
meanders in dreams
from nowhere to nowhere,
eddies and quiet backwater,
cold starlight swept downstream.

Ohio, Monongahela, Allegheny.

Crouched behind magazines
in Pittsburgh's hotel, I lost
myself to *Superman*
while parents, distraught,
searched the darkening wharf.

Whether to thrash or bless me—
that became the question
when, bleary eyed, I finally
laid my last comic down.
They blessed me.

Ohio, Monongahela, Allegheny.

Rivers come with memories,
branches dipping low,
caught by the current, swept
backwards, drawn down
and finally let go.

Anecdote by Firelight

Ignoring his curfew, a child makes himself invisible, eavesdrops on adults. His father speaks of threadbare clothes worn by a boy on a winter street in Pittsburgh. Something in the father's tone.... Firelight plays on the carpet, mottles the darkened room. Drinks recline in coasters. I swerved to a stop, the father says, rolled my window down, gave the boy money for shoes. Again the son notes a catch in the voice. The room falls silent except for shifting logs. He wonders at the silence, wonders at the plight of the needy boy and, years later, wonders why that scene unfolds like a dream...over and over again.

Pins and Combs

I watch her loose the pins and combs,
surprised again that so much hair falls
from her braid, tumbles the length
of her back. She props the window
with Grandfather's stick and we're down
on our knees, praying
the guardian angel prayer
and one that says, *if I should die....*

The chain on the bedside lamp clicks,
jounces there in the dark.
A dog barks, a car rumbles by
dragging slow lights down the wall.
Wind is in the curtain and I wonder what
would happen if I died before I woke.
Water seeps under the door, tugs
the legs of our bed. Somewhere at sea
a wave splits in half. Black
and trembling it plows toward me.

The Wish

1
Stillness echoes thrughout the house.
By a second-floor window
a gray-haired man, knees crossed,
nods over a book. Afternoon rays
slit by a louvered shade fill the room
with dusty spindles of dark and light.

Watching his father's eyelids fall,
the boy, unseen, flushes with power.
Hefting a primitive chant, he stalks
into the room:
Did you ever think when a hearse goes by...
poised now above the man's head,
that you may be the next to....
He wields the blunt rhyme, spins
at the stair post, drops three steps,
fires a glance back at strips of shin
and calf hung from folded knees.
The man has not stirred.

2
Flowers in vases of paper mache,
tiers of gladioli trailing gold-sequined
messages: *Sympathy, In Memory,*
relatives from distant towns
celebrating sorrow in the livingroom.

The boy escapes to his yard
past grade-school nuns hunched
in black habits, rosaries at the ready
for a homemade wake.
The apple tree, a trapeze branch,
he shinnies to the crook
snapping tags of bark. Upside down
he hangs by knees, red-faced.

Quiet Time

Sister Mary Gabriel
pats her fleshy palm
with a hard-edged
ruler, reminds us
the silence must
be absolute.

Hard at the stub
of a No. 2 pencil I've
gnawed way
down to graphite bone,
I'm squeezing tin
between my teeth,
coaxing dregs
of a worn eraser
up into the light.

Sister's black
leather shoe
squeaks behind me.
I lay the pencil down,
pry a thumbnail
off the quick.
Pink and moist
the half-moon skin
shies from the air,
throbs
with each thump
of my pulse.

Again the slow shoe...
I fold my hands
together—
church without a steeple—
sit still, absolutely
still.

Holy Writ

Study shows that 80% of primary teachers
unsure how to teach handwriting.
          ...The Tennessean (Nashville)

Back in the 40s the Sisters
of St. Joseph embraced
with great solemnity the sacred
vows of Poverty, Chastity
and the Palmer Method.

Sister Mary Raphael loved to teach
penmanship. When she spoke
in cursive, beads of spittle
iced her lips. Glaring out
from steel rims, she'd start
at 9:15 each day with ovals
on the blackboard. Scowls
and ovals over and over
until like slinky wire toys
they'd spill down on our desks,
fill our grainy paper
with undulating tunnels that
beckoned me inside, promising
a cubbyhole, a place
to crawl and hide myself
from fire-breathing dragons
and wild boars in heat.

Round-the-World

The man from Duncan Toys
came to school each spring
with dazzling exhibitions
of yo-yo pyrotechnics
and rhinestone gear.
Bursting loose at final bell,
we'd spot the make-shift stage,
the jet-black suit, the suede lapels
and flashing from his fingertips,
arcing from both hands—
spools of light, fine-spun orbs
circling a kinetic pole,
a magnetized spiderman
tossing crystal filaments
off the slanting sun.
His webwork fell around us,
held us there in awe.

The catechism taught us
seven *Cardinal Sins,*
but in second grade
I had to use imagination
to pin down *Lust.*
So I thought about the yo-yos,
the glittering gems.
The lust came later…
her name was Ginny Horner.
In a peasant blouse
with puffy sleeves,
she looped me to her finger,
snapped me up and down,
spun me round the world.

Picnic at Taughannock

1
Uncle Mike's Packard rounds a bend,
slams to a neck-snapping stop.
Doors swing out, the road-worn unfold.
Get the big hook, groans Nanna,
conjuring up a steam-powered crane
to muscle her out of her seat.
Mamie's bones crack and Ella won't budge
till she's covered the tips of her knees.

Stooping to clear their bonnets,
punching the air with canes,
they clamber off the running board
mad at Mike McCabe. Railroad retiree
with gold-filled teeth, he fancies himself
on a diesel, scorching the tracks from Sayre
to Lackawanna. Lizzie calls him
Leadfoot, snickers when he vows,
I'll drive this car till the day I die.
Bundled in wicker baskets: tablecloths,
napkin rings, silverware and salt.

Feathers preened, hats repinned,
they turn to my brother and me,
fuss at how we've grown. Heady
with approval, we wheel about their legs—
Ella's wrapped like a mummy's—
somersault and tumble
to their wide-eyed wonder
then tear away through bending grass
chasing wisps of wind.

2
Our white-haired clan came back
each June to this breezy picnic grove
that fronts Cayuga Lake. Grandparents,
aunts, great-aunts and uncles rose from

winter belfries, met the sun head-on
and fluttered down to benches
now blistered and pocked with age.

Facing a pebbled shore, they chat about
the weather, neighbors, the Mass:
Kate and Bert have taken a boarder,
says Nanna, mopping her mouth with
a kerchief. Lizzie strokes a pocketbook
curled in her lap, and Margaret winds
a wedding ring around a blue-veined finger.

3
From a float off-shore, we flag
our death-defying stunt—
a piggy-back plunge off the high board—
then swim underwater back
to the dock, hide like frogs. In shadows
that heave and echo, in pockets
green as caves, we cling to pilings
of slimy moss, giggle, bob and watch.

Nanna shifts, talking stops,
bonnets tilt our way. First Mamie
then others rise to sharpen their gaze.
Transfixed at water's edge, they scan
the sudden calm, then like a covey
flushed on cue, swirling about in fits
and starts, they ballyhoo the guard.
Dripping with glee, we scramble up
the ladder, whoop, jump and yell *Taa-Daaa!*

4
At dusk, when the lake flattens
and shadows lengthen the shore,
we search for stones, flat ones
made for the tossing finger,

learn ways to skip them sidearm.
From a tilted launch they veer, rip
the water, but on level flights we count
each   easy   leap
faster toward the end...seven-a-ni-ten...
when no one is sure in darkening mist
if the final beat is a splash...or not.

Verbal Tic

*I was dandering by
and says I, I might as well call.*
　　　...Seamus Heaney

She had an odd habit
of seasoning her thoughts
with, *So I said....*

Who'd you say it to? I'd ask.

In feigned exasperation
Grandmother would explain,
*So I said to myself,
to myself I says,
so I says to myself says I....*

We made ourselves a game—
if I flagged her *so-I-said's*
before she said her say,
she had to chant her jingle.
If I wasn't quick enough,
my query was lost
in the surge of conversation.

I loved that game,
the music of her lilt, the joy
of interrupting an adult.
But you had to be fast,
like pinning a crayfish
in startled retreat
before it slips back into silt.

Mess Hall

Wafting up the stairwell from our basement
cafeteria, oozing under classroom doors
like some noxious fog in a horror film,
those dreaded fumes announce
the day's lunch: sauerkraut.

The noon bell, the long gray line,
the single-file descent...down and down
into that building's reeking bowels, abandoning
hope on the way, I'm practicing lines like,
Thank you, that's plenty, praying
the hair-netted counter help will mercifully wave

my share. But I know too well my timid pleas
will be ignored, know I'll wince and gnash
my teeth as the lady with wattle under her arms
loads up a ladle with great steaming gobs
and shovels them down on my plate.

The iron-fisted commandant
of hell's eighth ring is Sister Mary Mavia.
Wider than a dumpster, she oversees
her mess hall infallibly, overrules
recess if we don't choke down every shred.

I gulp what I can till I start to gag, thumb
the rest down a milk carton's neck, fluffing my
napkin, a decoy distraction, in case she checks.
And check she does, nosing through dregs
like a big-boned hound. Lord have mercy
she's found my stash: *You will eat it...or no exit!*

Slouching back to my seat, I wait till she gnaws
at some other poor wretch, then muck
it into my socks, stuff it down into pockets
and slather it under my shirt, cursing—
for keeps—her sauerkraut soul.

The Lie: Seventh Grade

To the nuns' dismay, he liked
to make his classmates laugh
projecting ventriloquial grunts,
even in that English class taught
by his widowed mom.
It wasn't easy juggling roles
of class clown and loving son.

Once she asked why
the kids snickered so each time
she announced a pop-quiz.
He shrugged, shook his head,
played dumb. How to explain
such things to your mom,
words so sure to rock the room:
Clear your desks, class,
it's time for a quickie.

Sex Education: The Basics

The pastor imported a corps of shock troops,
brimstone cops with Roman necks
to execute our 8th grade retreat.
A quintessential sermon went like this:
"Walter was fondling his girlfriend
when his speeding car hit a patch of ice.
His funeral Mass was interrupted
when Walter cried out from fires of hell,
Father, it's no use!"

Dogs of guilt unleashed by flames
snapped at our heels with a vengeance.
Sammy and I quit the peeping elm
that laddered us up to Muffy's window.
Swearing he'd spill his seed no more,
Jim McKnight whacked into Ball jars.
Al Buranski just said no to self abuse
by slamming a window on his
wake-up erections. *Guillotine contrition,*
he said, boasting about it at school.

II.

Camping by the Klamath

I asked a lot of the river—
shade, shoals, deep pools—
spent most of yesterday
searching for perfect spots.
Here the flow too sluggish,
there the riffles dull.

This morning I just stayed put.
In a sandy cove where
overhanging creepers
and honeysuckle vines
retreated just enough to frame
the river, I watched it drift.

Mule deer waded the shallows,
an osprey circled pines overhead,
herons trod the far shore
and hatching damsel flies
bounced above a current
that muscled itself to the sea.

I just stayed put
and the river came to me.

Song of the Circular Saw

In strong wind the worn saw
down by the shed turns
with the slow tick of a spent
roulette. Tonight, again
in parka and watch cap
I cross the frozen pasture,
mistaking the wind in high thistles
for whispering cattle, drawn
again to unjawed teeth
all leaning in one direction.

What's to be done with a worn blade?
I knew the hands that built
this farm, planed
the lumber, oiled the saw
until it was not just a tool
anymore, but a friend
with time and stories that sang
on winter afternoons to seeds
beneath the snow. Fingers
riding burled oak into and past
the whine, sawdust pluming
down his back,
swifts on a darkening sky.

What's to be done with a worn blade?
I heft it, a discus,
and spinning like a dervish
launch it toward the sky.
It hovers a moment above the marsh
trailing bluish flame…
pasture and valley fall away,
it clears the last escarpment,
takes its place among the stars.

Wilderness

Branches burned to ash,
the dregs of an open fire curl
and snap at our feet.
Cocooned in down
we yield to dreams.
I'm driving a runaway bus,
hurtling down a rush-hour street,
passengers screaming,
brake gone straight to the floor.
The bus turns yellow,
my riders are kids.

Now the screams
are coming from children
here, in the woods.
They bring us both bolt upright.
Trembling, confused,
What is it? Where are they?
Cries like sparks flash
in darkness around us, tear
through boughs of Jeffrey pine
and ride the night winds out to sea.

Coyotes, I guess
as silence descends, though
they could have been children—
hungry, lean and wild.

Fishing with Frank

A black and red
inflatable raft
bobs us like puppets
above this mountain lake.
Draped over the bow,
he cradles the trout
in one hand, wriggles
his hook with the other,
slips it from cartilage
while the fat three pounder
strikes a ferocious pose.

He lowers it to water,
strokes its underside,
sets it free. Arcs
of morning sunlight
skip off droplets
from fish and hand,
form a beaded cord
strung
to something
silent and gentle
below
keeping our raft afloat.

Walking Stick

A woodland hike, I'm
rooting through vines,
poking at brush
and windfall limbs
for a branch, just so,
in length and heft.
The one I choose
still not right.
I grind both ends
on a rock, stomp
off the crook, peel
the blistered bark
to bone.

Habit grown to ritual—
a man, the woods,
a walking stick—
nothing remarkable here,
except the stick.

If I needed a pole
to scale some ridge
or brace a gimpy knee...
but the trail is flat,
legs are fine. Oh, I
use it now and then
to whack a weed's
prickly head or jab
a hollow stump
clear through,
but mostly it swings
at my side
solid and horizontal
just as it has
for thousands of years.

Turtle Project, Wassaw Island

Swept toward shore
on tides of May
a loggerhead turtle broke
from surf, plowed across
the dunes and laid her eggs.

Beside that silent cache
my daughter stands watch
while a fat August moon bleaches
live oaks along the shore.

Slowly at first
the nest begins to heave...
hairline cracks, rivulets
of sand and finally a cave-in
uproots the flailing life.

Flashlight in hand,
she scuffs away drifted wood
tangled knots of kelp,
beams the tiny hatchlings
back across the dunes.

At the edge of the oaks
a gray fox sniffs the wind,
watches them go.

Raptor

Early October, high in the Sierras, I climb
to keep pace with the sun, to balance it whole
on the last long ridge, to stay the coming night.
Walls across the canyon slowly gone to shadow...
my trail dead ends on a granite spine.
Small black lizards skid over scree.

On alpine winds a cruising hawk banks,
drops to track some hapless creature strayed
into his ken. Drumming wings to hang
in place, he drops again, strafes my roost
so close I can count the reddish-brown quills
speckling his white underside.

Having marked me well, he climbs once more,
cocks his claws, dives at my face. Shrunk
to a fetal tuck, I'm fanned by disdain.
He mounts a rising canyon draft and is gone.

The sun, instead of setting, simply quits the sky.
Jays chant vespers in manzanita shrubs
as I bed down on brittle duff. At 8,000 feet
the cold will find me long before sleep,
wind will sough the boughs of this pine,
and I will give in to the night, consent
to that part of the terrible dark that is mine.

Range War

The pasture snow, slush heavy
from yesterday's thaw
refroze last night. Tough-crusted
and glazed, it stutters
the hoof falls of white-faced Herefords,
buckles in ice-flow chunks
under a pickup truck. Bombardiers
in John Deere caps shove
bailed hay off a jangling tailgate,
block busting tufts of rye grass
that shiver and hide under
camouflage white. The herd,
fouling and bawling in grunts
and butts, zeroes in
on the first flung bale, ignoring
dozens more strewn down
a contrail of tread. Drubbing
each other for one mound
of fodder, they work their way
from payload to payload
until, at dusk, the commotion
subsides. When it snows
at night in the country
all you can see is the quiet.

Behavior: Two Views

A Steller's jay dead
out back. Gray cat
cuffs
it once or twice,
disappointed
there's no life. Mother jay
in the pine overhead
squawking out her rage...

or just squawking
and the cat just cuffing
and the bird just dead.

Catch and Release on the Bitterroot

Montana snowcaps catch the August sun,
skip it down a river where Frank and I
fish for brownies and rainbows. It shatters
on impact, splits the riffles with light.

We're old mule skinners lashing the air,
looping our lines back and forth to puff
the elk-hair fly. Mine shoots downstream
toward a dark green pool, hangs in a flutter

just above the flow, soft enough to summon
a shadow from the depths. Bursting
pink slams the fly, clamps its jaw
against my tug, yanks, leaps, dives.

Fins and muscle writhe in my grip, it
lurches free, slaps the boat's floor, refuses
to shed my hook. Released at last
it drifts, rolls, sinks to bitter roots.

At the Gibbon Cage

To the crowd's delight she jackknifes
through a swinging tire,
shakes her rump against the bars,
loop-de-loops a jungle gym
and lands with a toe in her mouth.

Now she grows still, turns to one side,
curses her lot with spasmodic cries,
huffing   winded   whooeee's
rising at the end to one convulsive
high-pitched scream that slams
us against the cage, whitens our joints,
makes us hang on for dear life
until her night is gone and we
slump back pretending it was funny.

Working the River

Who am I, if not one who listens
for words to stir from the silences they keep?
—Peter Everwine

Fishing below the dam,
I boat the oars of my rubber raft,
surrender to current.
Slow water and light wind
check my drift, suspend
the lure at tempting depths.

Downstream the flow fans me
sideways, to clover banks
favored by heron and deer.
Becalmed, I check for snags.

The drift resumes…
until an eddy, insistent, tugs
me upstream toward
the bend where I began.

So the morning deepens as I ply
this course, down and back,
down and back, working
the currents and winds.

Natural Selection

Cyclone fencing rims
Munich's airport,
sweeps the length of
frontage roads, runways.
Whorls of barbed wire—
spikes wrenched
in all directions—
crown the fence to shelter
travelers from acts of terror.
Tucked within those
jagged coils, a bird's nest.

From the Corner of My Eye

Belly to blanket and well out
of reach, she reads D. H. Lawrence
not wanting to distract me.

I like to write alone
by this mountain lake
but today she is here and her hair....

My desk a picnic bench splotched
with dried chalk from birds. Her back
slides down to her waist, hips curve....

A two-pronged needle from the pine above
spreads by my elbow while her thighs...
not wanting to distract me.

Afterlife on a Summer Night

A gangly daddy longlegs crazed
by light caroms off the porch bulb,
smacks the door and dives
into a bucket with kamikaze flare.
Unlike the water strider,
we called them water skeeters,
its stilt-high legs, all ankles
and knees, aren't made for skating,
it can't even swim. Buckling in
soggy knots, a tangle of noodles,
it sinks to the tub's floor where,
in slow motion, the legs disengage,
settle once again in perfect order.
A lithe mandala of limbs, it begins
to glow, pulsing yellowish orange
from cords of symmetrical grace.

•

Swarm

They found a hole in my stucco wall
where TV cables once snaked through,
moved queen mother in last June.
Now, late September, thanks to the ache
of pandering drones, their town
has grown by thousands. Fixed on juice
in distant fields, workers crowd
the exit. No false starts, no bumbling
back and forth, just flashes of light firing out,
clearing the shrubs at dizzy speeds.
Incoming flights loaded with sweets
stack like jets overhead.

Some dark night I could sneak out,
plug that hole, a cork would do.
Thoughts of Count Ugolino bid me pause.
Rusty bolts on tower doors imprisoned
his sons. Helpless, he watched them starve.
How long could my squatters feed
off their stores before they'd sack
that waxy comb, drill an inner wall,
swarm my bed?

Distracted by shrubs, neighborhood pines,
catbirds perched on the roof,
I barely give them a thought...except
when silence deepens the hum
and I think how brief the span—
weeks for workers, a year for drones,
two for the queen if she's lucky. A dull
murmur within—faint, low, finite.

III.

Wolves

Dwarfed by winter gales,
a juniper rooted in granite
marks the canyon headwall
where she wedged
herself away. Needles
and chips of drifted bark
sod her makeshift grave.

One grown runt—
maimed in her womb
and kept too long
at ready dugs—
comes by night
to circle her bones.
I have seen him
alone in the pines,
gaunt and lean in burdock,
tracking the wounded hare,
bent on a lame-eyed weasel.

Stone Pine

Elderberry leaves caught
the day's first light
long before I wakened
to find the crooked
tree out back
an old stone pine
with a sideways cant
had toppled

not from the crack
of lightning
or wrenching yank
of high winds
nothing dramatic like that
just a quiet concession
to forces below
bent on pulling it back.

The Closing

I hope you enjoy this house as much as I have.
..A.R.M

How often I think of that old man
who owned this house, who sat
out back in a lawn chair alone
with the roses and orange trees
as we, inside, muddled through
legal forms. His daughter and son,
well into middle age, hosted a broker
who briefed us on fuses, vents,
down payments, as they recalled
secret nooks and nuggets of family lore...
then back to the business at hand—
disclosures, waivers, multiple layers.

I watched him from the window,
a man I'd come to know through
life-prints left behind: the brownstone
ring surrounding the pine,
the kiln-baked bricks by the fish pond,
the mouse decal on a windowpane
and, tucked away in the shed,
a jar of colored stones, *Amy's Rocks.*
Lost in that whiteout of paper, we
dutifully signed *here...and here,*
just below the trembling script of
A-r-t-h-u-r R. M-c-C-a-s-k-i-l-l
(Seller).

Like cursive traced by a diligent child
bent on getting it right, his quivering loops
and curls were penned with great care.
I could feel the concentration packed
into that "A," the Celtic will that held
it to the line. But as the name played out,
the hand grew faint and letters began

to rise, drifting off on their own,
shorebirds in flight.

Something Belated

for PK

Quarantined by rain
we dogfight in the kitchen,
your Messerschmitt
bedecked with decals
strafes the cockpit of my P-38.
But the barrel-roll finale is aborted—
your mother sits us down
with sketchbooks, erasers,
pleas for peace.

Like cactus,
burr-headed stick men track
the desert of my page
gunning each other flat
with bullets the size of fruit,
while somewhere off the coast
of Madagascar
your oak-masted schooner rides
a charcoal storm.

Thunder on your wedding day.
Awaiting the bride, you're tossed
on waves of cold sweat, currents
of nerves, me at your brow.
Now she is gone. You tried
to call when snow was soiling
Manhattan and prophets
were sleeping on steam.
Connections failed.

Who needs belated hands?
Better this sketch by a stick man
shot through the chest with a plum.

Piper on Cayucos Pier

A gull's yellow eye fallen from flight,
perhaps a turban snail, skids
beneath a ledge of sand-ground stone.

Cornrows of mussels—tense, exposed—
cling to rocks for refuge, await
the tide's return, the rush of submersion.

Shoes in hand, I slosh through pools
off the central coast, late afternoon,
late October. A lone seal lolls

in fronds of swaying kelp.
Beyond the cries of downshifting gulls—
the wavering bleats of a bagpipe.

I flashback to pipers who rocked my pub
St. Patrick's Day. A merry band
in Scottish kilts. Yanks, Hispanics,

Asians, all honking and beeping
with gusto enough to curdle my stout.
Now, spotting the piper,

I watch him lead a solemn crew
down a pier adrift in haze.
Framed by oaks on rolling hills,

a sky draining crimson, one tilts
an urn, sows the sea with ashes.
Others join in a chorus of gesture.

Darkening clouds snuff the sun,
the gulls, the pier…consume their
fading hues, become the greater night.

The Lift

The chair swoops in like a great-clawed bird,
snatches you out of a fetal tuck, jounces
once and climbs on updrafts of cable
toward summits gone to mist.

Unlike the humming belts that shunt
air travelers from concourse to concourse
through neon caves—lost souls pass on left—
or escalating stairs at Macy's that rise

from scrublands of shoes, your lift skims
pines that bend to morning snow, ascends
to marble lakes and stilled moraine...
then nothing but suspension, the whistling cord

and your own huddled shadow passing
over earth, closing on a terminal, a ramp
where you'll alight, glide off on trails untracked
by grief, sloping toward meadows of powder
silence and light.

Chant

In darkness a tangerine tumbles through branches,
lands on a sculpted lawn. Winter rain spatters
the rind. Inside, a party swills on. Chatter flits
from stocks and bonds to sports and nouveau
boutiques. Gregorian chant, currently pop,
pounds from satellite speakers.

Niched into granite five thousand feet high,
into a hushed, wintry range north of Barcelona,
Trappist Monks intone psalms of compline,
antiphones at end of day. Chants rise
from wooden stalls, resound in Gothic arches until,
with hands sleeved, tonsures sheathed,
they bend in cowled silence beneath
the Dark Madonna, pray for souls departed.

Purgatory

Bent on hurling themselves yet again
off a spongy diving board clamped
to the roof, a giddy procession of nudists
corkscrews up the lighthouse steps.
Anxiously waiting their turns, they clap
with glee as souls ahead vault into space.
A free-fall of howls and windmilling limbs,
the airborne plunge to depths below where,
in manic haste, they flail toward shore,
scramble up mossy rocks to join
the queue again and again.
For listening delight, rock, rap and jazz
blast through the stairway. In plaster masks
with identical grins, purgatory's inmates—
condemned to insatiable play—
cleanse themselves of their sins.

Pilgrimage to a Georgia Prison

—in memory, Francis McMahon (1838-1915)
POW, Andersonville, GA

Our family reunites to visit your prison,
a *National Site* complete with maps and guides.
Flanked by magnolias, spring-burst azaleas,
the sound of soughing branches in the pines,
I try to comprehend the squalor.
Forty-five thousand men and two women
marched in turn from a railroad yard to gates
of a pine stockade. Disgorged on facing hillsides,
did you wonder at cries of *Fresh fish?*
Schooling like cod to protect yourselves,
you were scaled of clothes by Yanks who preyed
on their own, who clubbed and maimed
for shoes, as hollow skulls looked on.

You fashioned a pup tent, a buffer against
winter rains and pounding August sun,
a patched shebang of oil rags, coats
and frayed blankets. Shrouds of friends
were also used after scurvy puffed their gums,
flushed their teeth away. Your poles were
wobbly sticks from the same Georgia forest
they razed on backs of slaves for walls
squared and planted side by side by side.
Daily rations: a crusted snarl of bread—
corn-laced dough seasoned with husks—
and occasional globs of cowpeas,
all you could grab with one hand.

Face blackened by fires of gristly wood,
you had to draw water from a sluggish stream
that oozed through a marsh, a quagmire of shit
and decomposed slime teeming with maggots
and flies. Sweetwater Creek, the camp latrine,
spawned flies for your sores, flies for your bread,

flies for your face as you slept,
flies for gangrenous wounds of friends
and slack-jawed mouths of the dead.

Did you know a David Kennedy,
9th Ohio Cavalry? He penciled a note
that somehow escaped: *It takes
7 of us ocupiants to make a Shadow.*
Dysentery, scurvy, diarrhea and starvation
won sweet release for hundreds each day
whose bones hummed in graves of mud.
Did you know about the women? Surely
there were rumors. One, Florena, mustered in
with a man blown into limbs of a Shiloh tree.
Her sister-in-arms and 13,000 *ocupiants*
never left that stockade alive.

Lulled by the stillness of April's afternoon,
I picture the sweet-gums and willows that may
have lined the stream before pilings
slowed it to a swamp, picture raccoons
and spotted skunks padding down their nightly
haunts. Little Susie flowers dot the bank
at my feet and crows in a distant tulip tree
kick up a fuss over God knows what.
Their rage and a knee-high sign sunk into moss—
DANGER SNAKES—are all that hint of the chaos.

Hobgoblin

We bought sweet corn, a dozen ears.
Girls at the roadside stand tossed in a spare.
I'm shucking them now, too fussy, I know,
about the fine silk floss tucked within the rows.

Thumbing through Christmas cards, you
were three, we guessed orange juice
and pacifiers must have been gifts of the wise men.
One was named King Friday, you ventured,

Mr. Rogers' friend.

After I left, we sometimes met on a farm like this.
They called it *quality time.* You were six
and loved to knead the cords that line
my neck singing a favorite rhyme,

Crisscross, applesauce, tight squeeze, cool breeze!

A puff of air to the back of my neck flushed
a gaggle of chill bumps. And days were a wash
if we didn't play cards, especially Hobgoblin,
that game with silly ghouls, except for him —

a warty, yellow-eyed gnome.
Woe to the hand stuck with that beast.
The hands have changed. You have grown,
so have I…and so has he.

Elkhorn Slough: Monterey Bay

Plowing through swells of night fog,
the restaurant at Elkhorn Slough rides
its pilings like a ghost ship.
Bluish light spills from the deck, profiles
a pelican roosting on a piling of its own.

On a rickety porch, I breathe salt air.
Muffled lights on a barge below
meld into darkness deep as canyons
that ballast the bay. Family and friends
chat inside at our window table.

We'd spent the afternoon in kayaks,
sculling our way up the narrowing slough,
bucking an outgoing tide. Bug-eyed seals
surfaced about us and fat sea otters lounging
on their backs cracked open clams with stone tools.

Amused by my airy perch, I call
to my crew, wave in clownish gestures
but glass and mist double my remove.
They cannot see or hear me.

A hairsbreadth away, this foursome
that glows at my planet's core—
daughter, wife, and life-long friends—
leans first towards one, then another:
smiles, nods, bursts of laughter.

Hovering out over water, on the dark side
of the window's glare, I can almost hear
them breathe, almost touch their hands
and I suddenly know the flickering time
when presence and absence will be like this.

Drawn back by joy as well as grief,
I will return, will be unseen.

Then I'll remember this night, say I have made
such visits before. Then I'll remember
the slough, the foghorn out on the bay.

The Will

He wants to be entombed in a sandbox
where his ashes can laze with shovels,
dump trucks, brightly-colored rakes.

He wants a tent to dome the box,
to keep the ashes dry. In time, he says,
the dome will sag, become a pool

for summer rain, a bath for sparrows
and wrens, a pond to tempt the Cooper's hawk
from beams of neighboring pines.

He wants some ashes saved
for the deck of a model boat
like those sold at hobby shops.

He'd have it launched from a grassy bank
where eddies, lazy at first, swerve
to rapids hellbent on a falls.

Taughannock Falls will do.
In tumbling whitewater he'll vault
off a ledge two hundred feet high, hang

a second till raw momentum explodes
into glorious freefall, spawning
winds of its own, coursing down and out

a thin white veil diffusing
at the fringes into far-flung mist.

Cayuga Lake

1
Distant thunder, the spatter of vanguard rain,
mist webbing treetops along the western shore—
these are the gods who come each June
to consecrate Cayuga's glacial scar.

2
Scrub grass of summer snaps underfoot
as I pick my way past gravestones, inlaid photos
of loved ones. U.S. flags on tiny sticks cordon
off the HEARSON plot, latest arrival: MATTHEW,
the town's crack mortician who buried my
parents three decades apart. Then a five-foot
column of granite etched with our family's name.

Flush with the grass eight small plaques flank
the larger stone. Three remain uncut. I pry
a blade from my pen knife, drop to my knees
and mindlessly chisel at lichen caked inside
an "M." For a moment it seems important.

3
High on South Hill I scan the steepled skyline,
trace the fall of Aurora Street out to the lake
where tiny sails catch a breeze, turn it white.
Tightroping over Buttermilk's gorge, tracks
deadhead for Morris Chain—a crow's nest
of commerce shaded by trees where workers
at lathes called my grandfather boss.

We scaled those trees, my brother and I,
to ogle the typists in swivel seats.
Towheaded voyeurs, we dangled by knees
and jingled, *Hubba hubba ding ding....*
The blonde by the cooler laughed and blew
us kisses. And down the green of summer
we hiked the tracks, teetering atop the rails,

hopscotching over the ties.

4
Sunrise breaks off the eastern hills.
The lifeguard roost at Taughannock Park
is still asleep. I stroll the pebbled shoreline,
watch mist rise off the lake and think of
the house on Hillview Place gone to strangers
long ago.… In a cane-back rocker, Mother
and I press our brows together, close our
eyes and count: *one…two…three…OWL!*
The *owl* pops our lids. I cannot wait to
start again, to synchronize the count
with the chair's slow grind.

Across the den, neatly framed, she and her
groom pose on a carpet gilding
a terraced lawn. Enchanted by the wedding
pomp, they center themselves with a smile.
So I center them now on their magic rug
just above the lake. They bask in light from
the other shore, a gentle kind of brightness
borne on summer wind.

Rewrite Man

in memoriam JFM (1903-1950)

1

Local reporter for *Evening Times* accepts position with *New York Sun.*
The Evening Times, Sayre, PA. May 1, 1929

A paper trail, boxed away in the '50s, unearthed
by a son who tracks his dad through time.
Letters, photos, clippings. By their snippets ye shall know them.
A faded notebook with lines from *Ozymandias,*
quotes from St. Jerome on the Apocalypse
and smatterings of word play—*black moss, black mask,*
black Mass—along with repetitions of a young teacher's
name, Ruth. The Great Depression's impact
on the *New York Sun* transforms the cursive into gloom:
Outlook bleak. Out of work. No place to turn.

2

**Former reporter for *Evening Times* appointed night editor for the
Associated Press in Pittsburgh.** *The Evening Times,* Sayre, PA. June 22,
1932

On the graveyard shift, he's sculpting facts in paragraphs
for a grimy steel city, scouring Teletype for newsdom's
tale of the day. Amid the din of jangling phones
and deadline cries for copy, he snitches time to bang out
missives on a beat-up Royal to Ruth. Every night.

*One picture, so vivid in my mind. When I arrived, you'd been
napping out back. You came to the door sleepy-eyed. I never saw
you just waking before, and can't forget how lovely you looked.
I stole a kiss, half expecting to be caught. Later, I learned we
were alone. Had I known that, it wouldn't have been just one.*

After work he and a colleague wind down with a *crock*—
their call for bonded rye. Eggs at White Tower and home by dawn.

3
**Former reporter for *Evening Times* lands executive slot with
Mellon's Industrial Hygiene Foundation in Pittsburgh.**
The Evening Times, Sayre, PA. Feb. 18, 1936

Family man at mid-career, he pens Ruth, his wife, a *missive:*
June has been frantic. In the rush to clear his desk, to join his family
visiting Sayre, he has *hit the ball hard.* Endless rounds with chemists,
job candidates and a D.C. trip for a keynote speech.
Proud of his suburban home far from smog's ground zero,
he adds a dash of household news—skunks beneath the porch,
a downed tree, and curses on the neighbors for burning trash:
That clan has scorched our hedge again, the lugs.

4
**Former reporter for *Evening Times* suffers heart failure at his desk,
dies at age 47.** *The Evening Times*, Sayre, PA. Sept. 15, 1950

An agent of industrial health, he's briefing the press
on poisonous gas spewed by mills south of Pittsburgh.
A deadly smog in Donora, PA, will snuff the lives of dozens.
One news photo captures him and his tools—paperclips,
tapered pens, ash trays bristling with matches and butts.
Thanks to the camera's angle, the photo is mirrored
in the glass desk top. His striped tie appears, and just above
the tie his neck's reflection meets the desk's edge
and stops.

Requiem

I did not fall to my knees or hurl
myself on your grave, but turned into
a crow and mocked the blind archangels.
Potted plants shouted threats,
said I must be still.

Too bad there were no stallions
to pull your hearse, no Irish hounds
with shaggy hair to trot along behind
like one you had when you were young...
I never can think of his name.

I dreamt about a requiem,
some strange beach. Hermit crabs
found you clutching your beads.
They pierced your side with mussel shells,
crowned you with kelp. Communion
for family only. I blessed myself, rose

from the sand, conscious of being watched.
Pumped for drama, something a little
wrenching, my classmates looked on.
Kneeling tall in driftwood pews,
they tried to please the nuns.
Plovers wept, gulls patrolled the aisles,
gowns ballooned in the wind.

Marian Manor

Sunday guests clumped about the lounge,
nurses and nuns on the prowl.
In the vestibule gladioli feel the heat,
droop without shame.

We try the deck's wicker chairs.
Sunbaked tile burns our feet.
She fumbles for words
as if they were switches across a dark room.
It'll come to me later, she says,
tonight when I'm lying in bed.

I mop my brow, pluck at my shirt,
track the scuffing of slippered feet.
To cool me, as she did the steaming broth
lifted to my lips in winter's kitchen,
she blows a thin jet of air
up and down my neck.

Night Places

Where have we been when the rest home's
lounge bristles with blackened roses
and nuns with plaster smiles
foul our dreams and burst into flames?

Where have we been
when the morning light snuffs
those flames that make so little difference
to fields and barns beyond the woods,

to the underside of the sparrow's wing,
to the railroad bridge with hollow ties
that hasn't been used in years.

Kilrush, County Clare

The shop in Kilrush
is poorly lit. It smells of musk
and rubber boots. Shirts,
fertilizer, paint and detergents
all somehow at peace.
Cable-knit sweaters
on a cluttered shelf catch
my mother's eye. She wants
one for me. *Here, feel,*
the shopkeeper says. I dig
my hand down into wool,
past the dye that brands
the sheep, sets them off
from neighboring flocks,
past the dermis of natural oil
that helps them bear mizzling rain,
raw Atlantic storms,
past the bogs and bracken
west of Kilrush—all the way
down to the echo of my
own footsteps roaming
her empty house
after the movers have gone.

Once Again to Lisdoonvarna

in memoriam RBM *(1904-1984)*

1
She loved to work in the yard
pruning the rhododendron,
removing spent bulbs and sharing
with neighbors histories of shrubs
whose roots were so entwined
with her own it was hard
to distinguish the two. Touching
a sprig of quince, she'd speak
of its great migration
from a field behind her father's
home in Trumansburg, New York,
of his own harsh uprooting
from County Roscommon...
then back to the quince
and the year she was wed.

I helped her chop the elm
arched above her drive,
a wand of summer shade
gone brittle and combed with blight.
She spoke of days in school,
the let's pretend of an only child
pushing an empty swing.
A late September sun
warmed the trampled lawn.
I counted thunks of my axe,
thought of the fire
inside the wood, how it escapes
through friction. She clipped
the smaller branches.
It never seems as hard,
she said, *when there are two.*

2
Christmas over, I'd packed

the trunk, gone inside to say
good-bye and found her at the table,
smoothing out a map,
a souvenir of country roads
traveled long ago. Tracing the lines
as if they were braille, she took
me in her memory once again
to Lisdoonvarna, Connemara, Kilrush.
I had to be off before it snowed.

Small steps walked me to the car.
Dwarfed by the spruce Dad planted
in the 40s, she hunched
her back against the wind. That
was last I'd see her...except
for times when morning light
spills headlong into its own reflection,
and shrubs behind my house begin to blaze.
Then she drifts to the center
of my rearview mirror,
one arm at her side, the other
shoulder high, waving.

The Silent Ones

Could we exist without them?
R. M. Rilke

I love the ones who have gone and the way they are here with me, lending a hand at the wheel, watching the road when I sleep. How do I pay them back?

I love the silence they keep, like breath one never hears, like the silence of bark and its sweet underside. And their sense of humor, the laughter that swirls just out of reach like wind above the cathedral. And their easy trust, forgiving me over and over, remembering how it was.

I love the times to come when together we'll laugh as one says, *Remember that night you grabbed for the branch and it held? That was me.*

Acknowledgments

The author wishes to thank the editors of the following journals and anthologies in which some of the poems in this collection, or earlier versions of them, originally appeared:

Acorn Whistle	"Once Again to Lisdoonvarna"
Albatross	"Raptor"
Atlanta Review	"Round-the-World"
Blue Arc West: An Anthology of California Poetry	"Elkhorn Slough: Monterey Bay"
Blueline	"Stone Pine," "Wolves"
Buffalo Spree	"Fishing with Frank"
California Quarterly	"Natural Selection," "Hobgoblin"
The Comstock Review	"Cayuga Lake," "The Will"
The Hiram Poetry Review	"Pins and Combs," "Song of the Circular Saw," "Turtle Project, Wassaw Island"
Interim	"Range War"
Kansas Quarterly	"At the Gibbon Cage"
The Midwest Quarterly	"Pilgrimage to a Georgia Prison," "Swarm"
Natural Bridge	"Headwaters"
Notre Dame Review	"Chant," "Purgatory"
Pearl	"Behavior: Two Views"
Plainsong	"The Silent Ones"
Poet Lore	"Chalmers Lane," "Night Places"
Poetry East	"The Lift"
Poetry Now	"Something Belated"
RE Arts & Letters	"Holy Writ"
Seneca Review	"Picnic at Taughannock"
South Coast Poetry Journal	"Quiet Time"
Spoon River Poetry Review	"Camping by the Klamath," "Kilrush, County Clare"
Stone Country	"From the Corner of My Eye"
White Heron	"Wilderness"
Wind Literary Journal	"The Wish"
Wisconsin Review and Yosemite Poets: A Gathering of This Place	"Walking Stick"

Mike McMahon was born and raised in Pittsburgh, PA. After receiving a B.A. in English from the University of Notre Dame, he taught high-school English before earning his Ph.D. at the University of Pittsburgh.

His first academic appointment was at the University of Virginia, where one of his students submitted a poem in lieu of a required paper. That poem sparked a born-again conversion to the writing life. Mike resigned from his tenured position and embarked upon an odyssey of blue collar jobs on a horse farm, a tobacco factory and a D.C. Metro bus, which he drove four years.

After he and his wife moved to Fresno, CA. Mike returned to teaching. His students were Hispanic farm workers who met for evening classes in churches and homes. Drawn to the outstanding poets at CSU Fresno, he completed an M.A. in Creative Writing mentored by Philip Levine, Peter Everwine and Connie Hales. After years of teaching at Fresno Pacific University, he and his wife moved to the San Francisco area where they currently reside.

Mike's poems appear in anthologies and literary journals including the *Atlanta Review, Blackbird, Comstock Review, Notre Dame Review, Poetry East* and *Seneca Review.*

www.ingramcontent.com/pod-product-compliance
Lightning Source LLC
Chambersburg PA
CBHW021159090426
42740CB00008B/1162